A New Approach
to Academic Administration

A New Approach
to
Academic Administration

ELLIS L. PHILLIPS, JR.

President
Ellis L. Phillips Foundation

TEACHERS COLLEGE PRESS

Teachers College, Columbia University, New York

Cover Design by June Martin

This book was set by a Lintron 1010 cathode ray
tube composer in connection with a IBM 360 Computer.

Manufactured in the United States.

Foreword

The Ellis L. Phillips Foundation has been in operation since 1930, but few people in higher education heard of it until the early years of the present decade. After several years of preparation, Ellis L. Phillips, Jr., who had succeeded his father as president of the Foundation, launched the Program of Internships in Academic Administration in the summer of 1962. Soon the Foundation became known among young scholars with administrative careers directly or peripherally in mind. Soon, too, administrators in leading colleges and universities became associated with the Program as nominators of candidates for internships or as hosts to the young men and women selected to work for a fully-financed year under their direction.

During the eight years that Mr. Phillips served as assistant dean of the Columbia School of Law, and especially during his three years as Director of the Columbia University Budget, he became increasingly aware of the growing complexities of academic administration. This led him to the conclusion that no problems facing American higher education have greater urgency than the discovery and training of able administrators. Thus with the hearty approval of his fellow trustees of the Foundation, he initiated the internship plan to meet the problem which he so clearly recognized.

In this short, well-packed book Mr. Phillips not only describes the plan from its conception through its four years of functioning, but he also puts into historical and conceptual perspective the methods employed to find and equip men and women for positions of academic leadership. What he has written, therefore, constitutes both a report of the successful program which he initiated and an important review of the evolution of academic administration. Beyond doubt, it will become a widely used source book for students of this extremely important topic.

But that is not all. This book modestly records how a small foundation under perceptive leadership identified a crucial problem, mounted a plan to help solve it, and thereby set in motion the forces which activated a larger foundation to continue the plan on a larger scale. Thus the Phillips Foundation Program of Internships in Academic Administration has evolved into the larger internship program which the American Council on Education conducts.

W. H. Cowley
David Jacks Professor of Higher Education
Emeritus
Stanford University

August 1969

Introduction

Since 1940 we have witnessed such change that we have a hard time keeping a sense of perspective. The fantasies of Buck Rogers and Superman are now reported in the press releases of NASA and the prospectus of COMSAT. *Ulysses* is a movie, released for general distribution. A chronicle of the 1930's, such as Malcolm Cowley's *Think Back on Us*, reads like an account of the Peloponnesian Wars. We can measure the degree of change in our standard of wealth. Total government taxes collected on this wealth have passed the $200 billion mark, double the amount collected only ten years earlier. Total government expenditures in the United States are now estimated at $250 billion. The comparable figure in 1941 was less than $35 billion.

Our total annual product utilizing private and public wealth is approaching $900 billion. Perhaps the most dramatic use we have made of this new wealth is in building a system of higher education of unprecedented size and scope. Five million full-time students are now enrolled in American colleges and universities. This figure is expected to reach 8,000,000 by 1973. More students attend public and private colleges and universities in one state—Illinois—than in England, Ireland, Sweden, Norway, and Denmark combined. It is estimated that new junior colleges will be established across the country at the rate of 30 each year for the next quarter-century.

Education at all levels has become the leading growth industry in the United States. Expenditures for education from all sources total in the range of $45 to $50 billion each year—and the amount is increasing. Instead of the age of the atom or the computer, we may look back, in our time, on "the age in which the university became an institution for the common man." We have done so much in higher education in such a relatively short time that the problems associated with running our colleges and universities are difficult to understand, let alone solve. The problems and opportunities facing our academic leaders today call for a new approach to administering our colleges and universities in a time of rapid and pervasive change.

Contents

Foreword   v

Introduction   vii

I.   Perspective on Administration   1

II.   The Program of Internships   9
       in Academic Administration

III.   Education in Academic Administration   19

IV.   The Interns Speak Out   29

V.   Proposals to Clarify and Strengthen   37
       Academic Administration

       Appendix   51

". . . If our colleges and universities deteriorate, it will be because they lacked the morale, the internal coherence, and the adaptiveness to meet the requirements of the future; it will be because in the moments of their greatest success they could not pull themselves together to face new challenges."

—John W. Gardner
Address to the California Teachers Association Annual Conference on Higher Education, May, 1965, entitled "Agenda for the Colleges and Universities."

I

Perspective on Administration

The traditions of the present-day American college or university go back in part to the European continental university of which Bologna and Paris were examples by the end of the twelfth century, and of which the great sprawling Sorbonne is an example today. At various times these European continental universities have been governed by the students (as the guilds of scholars at Bologna), by the faculty (as the guilds of masters at the University of Paris), and by the state. At the Sorbonne today there is a large student body with loose affiliation with the university. The lecture system prevails. In terms of the number of students enrolled, facilities are limited. The university is a study center, a point of attraction for the student age group, rather than a distinct organic educational corporation as we think of colleges and universities in the United States. This European continental tradition is mirrored in many ways in the great universities of Latin America, but the reflection can also be seen today in North American campuses.

Our institutions of higher education also owe a debt of history to the English university. Oxford and Cambridge, the prime examples, enjoy a loose university government under a chancellor who may be a member of the royal family or nobility with only ceremonial responsibilities, and a vice chancellor, the equivalent of the American college president, who is appointed for a relatively short period of time and who, again, has much less executive responsibility than his American academic counterpart. The basic functioning unit of the British university is the college, to which master and student are called, at which they live, and to which is given the private (and more recently, the public) financial support which has helped make Oxford and Cambridge great centers of learning.

The North American college or university is also a product of our own history. Since 1636 when John Harvard made the first grant to higher education in the Colonies, we have sponsored a surprising

1

number of colleges, often at first with the vocational objective of training ministers or teachers, but soon after for broader purposes of civic and community leadership. The elements of present-day college and university authority in the United States were present from the beginning: the state charter, the trustees or regents, the president, the faculty, to some degree an organized unit of the educational corporation, and the individual students, constituting a generally unorganized student body. Until recently the small size of the average college or university and its simplicity of purpose, to teach and to sponsor scholarly research, enabled presidents to exert leadership directly upon and in close consultation and communication with the faculty and students. This remained true even after the introduction in the 19th century of the German idea of the importance of pursuing learning and research at levels beyond the bachelor's degree. Parallel with the addition of graduate training culminating with the degree of Doctor of Philosophy was a trend to associate professional schools with the college and graduate departments in the university structure. For example, the first American law school at Litchfield, Connecticut, transferred to New Haven and became part of Yale University. In New York City the College of Physicians and Surgeons became a part of Columbia University.

Scientific training at the level of higher education was greatly stimulated by the Morrill Act of 1862, which provided federal aid in the form of land grants to state universities. Schools of engineering were established at institutions such as Cornell University. Institutes of technology came upon the American scene, some of which, like the Massachusetts Institute of Technology, have in effect become universities. At the highest levels of research and training, there has been a recent renewal of the idea of a purely graduate institution. Rockefeller University has changed from a research institute into a center for graduate and postgraduate instruction and research in the biological sciences. Other examples are the Institute for Advanced Study in Princeton, N. J., and a proposed Institute for Science and Technology, to be organized and based in northern New Jersey and which has among its purposes:

close association . . . in this new center between industrial and academic scientists so that the process of education will be aided and students will gain a deep and early appreciation of the relationships between science and technology so crucial to our "scientific age".[1]

At the pre-bachelor level we have seen the emergence of two-year colleges, a twentieth-century educational phenomenon, as a major component of the system of higher education in America. California has formally decided to extend education for all through the thirteenth and fourteenth "grades" in the junior college. Many other states are now establishing junior or community colleges as fast as possible.

Since World War II there has been a boom in higher education without parallel in history. Traditional state universities and the more recently chartered state colleges have opened their doors to a flood of entering students. For example, the University of Minnesota now has nearly 40,000 students on its Minneapolis-St. Paul campuses; Ohio State University has a comparable number of students at Columbus; and in the State of California there are nearly 300,000 students involved in public higher education at some level.

While striving, sometimes without sufficient success, to give attention to the individual student, our colleges and universities comprise the fastest-growing portion of the leading growth industry in the United States. Education at all levels of schools and colleges now takes more than 33 billion dollars each year, and when the amount spent on education in industry, defense, and other governmental agencies is added in, the total annual bill is now running between 45 and 50 billion dollars. This would probably exceed the outlay for defense, were it not for the Vietnam war.

In California the master plan for higher education, which has been approved by the State Legislature, projects an enrollment of 600,000 full-time students at the junior college, college, and university levels by 1972.[2] Our state universities have long participated in special types of adult education, particularly in the area of agriculture. Now they are getting into all phases of continuing education for adults. Recently at the University of New Hampshire the first Regional Center for Continuing Education was established with a grant of $1,800,000 from the Kellogg Foundation. This center will serve six New England state universities and the citizens of those states. Within a year from the founding of the regional center, the first international conference on comparative adult education was held at Portsmouth, New Hampshire.

The private sector of American higher education has expanded as resources permitted. Although now educating considerably less than half of the total college enrollment, our privately supported institutions have benefited from the rush of students seeking entrance and the inflow of public funds for research and, more recently, for support of new programs and facilities.

There has been a constant effort to improve the quality of higher education. The four-year colleges have sought to retain and renew the old concept of unfettered, intense undergraduate liberal arts education which may be smothered in the great universities with their increasing emphasis on graduate instruction, research, scientific and technological development, and public and community service. Within the last ten years "new colleges" have been introduced: for example, at Hofstra on Long Island, at Sarasota in Florida, and recently at Hampshire College near the University of Massachusetts. The new colleges have very limited enrollments. The structure is one of freedom from departmental divisions, and the aim is to reestablish the old relationship between master and students. There is to be none of the paraphernalia that has grown up about the traditional college and university — no football teams, no stadia, no heavy emphasis on extracurricular events, no extension programs, nothing to divert student and master from the pursuit of the liberal arts in scholarly association.

At the traditional undergraduate and graduate levels of instruction, the urge for an international dimension in higher education grows stronger, adding to the burden of academic administration. On one side of the ledger a recent report notes that 275,000 U. S. students were studying abroad during 1967.[3] The legion of foreign students studying in the United States grows annually.

Society more and more turns to its colleges and universities for practical help on minority problems, urban affairs, and such programs as the war on poverty. Developments such as these, however desirable in response to the needs of society, extend the attention of our universities and their officers from existing business to a bewildering array of new areas of service. The pressures for growth and change in our educational institutions show no signs of abating, and the means to deal effectively with these pressures remain elusive.

The standard theory of organization of a college or university in America today begins with the board of trustees. In the private institutions the board may be self-perpetuating except for representatives of the alumni and occasionally of other groups. In the case of the public institutions, the board may be elected by the people, as in Illinois and Michigan, or appointed by the governor or elected by the legislature, as in the State of New York. Public or private trustees hold title to the property of the institution and are legally responsible for everything that goes on within its walls. In this sense the American trustees *are* the college or university.

At Berkeley in 1964 and more recently at Columbia and several other great private universities, groups of students acted to assert an ancient prerogative to a voice in the affairs of the college or university. This has resulted in a confrontation between the administration, as agents of the trustees or governing board, and the activist student organization. In this situation the faculty is in the middle, torn between an interest in students and their aspirations, in academic freedom, and concern for the integrity of the institution.

The New York Times on October 12, 1966, reported direct action by a few City College students in New York to halt construction of a parking lot on a wooded lawn which was favored by students for sun-bathing and sports activities. The article noted that the same students have also opposed the erection of prefabricated steel classrooms on another lawn. The objectors, who apparently acted outside of the student government, were successful in causing President Buell G. Gallagher to call a halt to the disputed construction until he could meet with them. Even more dramatically, in 1969 other students closed down City College in an attempt to force a new admissions policy.

In this instance the administration was seeking to carry out an assignment from the City University and Board of Higher Education to accept more students on a crash basis. Some of the students refused to put up with the inconvenience which resulted from the necessary physical changes to the campus. The question resolved, as it always does, into, "Who is running City College?" If the students, either in splinter groups or in student government, are to have a right of veto over administrative decisions, the implications are serious because responsibility will be diffused and decisions will change with student whim. The challenge to college and university administrators in adjusting to the role of the student in American colleges and universities today is a perplexing one. As Fred M. Hechinger, Education Editor of *The New York Times,* reported after attending the spring 1966 meeting of the Association for Higher Education in Chicago,[4] "University administrators, having rediscovered their students, are not sure what to do about them."

Beset by pressures for change from without and within the university community, academic administrators have seen the financial security of their institutions eroded in a time of great national prosperity. The more vocal critics of academic policy have tended to leave finance and fiscal control to the "experts." The Winter 1964 issue of *Columbia College Today,* in an article concerning the great growth in the financial budgets of our colleges and universities, notes:

It is precisely on this point—finances—that education is running into the most trouble. Teachers are in short supply and so are buildings, but money is even shorter. While Americans are demanding a powerful new emphasis on education, they are sometimes bafflingly reluctant to recognize the costs of such demands.

There are many examples of this resource squeeze. In New York City the press recently aired the question of financing the city colleges and the City University so that they can expand their enrollments while maintaining the quality of their services. A great many Americans have been involved in fund raising for colleges and universities and know first-hand both the hard work involved and the gratifying response to the well considered presentation of the needs of these institutions. Some of the strong state institutions rely heavily on typically private sources of support. A recent report of Ohio State University, for example, reveals that only about one-quarter of the operating expenses were charged to general revenues from the taxpayers of Ohio. Thirteen per cent came from student fees, a little over one per cent from endowment, and the balance, from public and private grants for research, sales and services, and auxiliary enterprises.

The largest new source of funds for public and private higher education is federal appropriations. As was pointed out in an article by Humphrey Doermann, then Admissions Director of Harvard College,[5] the support the federal government extends to higher education is for the first time exceeding such support from the state governments. This money is flowing into higher education from the federal government not only to support research and development, as has been the pattern since World War II, but now in the 1960's for facilities and equipment and most recently for general support of certain institutions. Unless there is a severe recession in the national economy, federal support of higher education will continue to increase in amount and widen in scope. The best evidence suggests that despite the increase in support of higher education from private gifts, from state appropriations, and now from the federal government, the level is not adequate to meet the demand for increased services in higher education and that the pressure upon our colleges and universities to spend wisely through fiscal planning and fiscal control will become greater than ever before.

The *Wall Street Journal* of April 28, 1966, noted in a lead column the desire of the administration in Washington to encourage program planning and budgeting, not only in the Defense Department where it was introduced under Secretary McNamara, but in other departments of the federal government. Consideration of similar budget planning techniques in colleges and universities is just beginning. In June, 1965, a conference, "Planning for Effective Resource Allocation in Universities," was sponsored by the American Council on Education at Woods Hole, Massachusetts. The participants discussed with representatives of the Rand Corporation (which has assisted in developing budget techniques for the Defense Department) and representatives of the American Council how a college or university might develop new ways of charting its overall mission and then determine how best to allocate available resources to these ends. It is the hope of proponents of "program budgeting" that college and university officers will have available to them, as elements of planning, all the costs of what they are undertaking to do and can understand the alternatives which are available within the limits of available financial resources.[6]

"Hope for the best" procedures and policies will not be financially feasible in the future. Colleges and universities can become financially embarrassed and may be forced to turn over all or part of their facilities to the state or to cease operations entirely. Our top college and university officers are learning that understanding how colleges and universities are financed is too important a question to be left to businessmen on boards of trustees or to specialists in the academic community, such as vice presidents for business and finance, business officers, and controllers. All top educational leaders, including those with primary orientation to traditional academic disciplines, must make it their business to understand the elements of financial support and administration and enough of the jargon of accounting and fiscal control to be able to participate in preparing the financial budgets and reports of their institutions and to make the financial judgments called for.

The problems of administering colleges and universities have their roots in the beginnings of these institutions and are looming large today since higher education has boomed into the greatest "growth industry" in America. Our society is the first to set its sights on mass education at the college level, and on top of this requirement it seeks to use the college or university to solve many of its general problems. The resulting pressures for growth and change come down particularly hard on college presidents, whose power is only delegated from their trustees and must be shared, now as formerly, with faculty and students. Presidents and their colleagues in administration have plenty of advice on running the academic show, but when it comes to accepting responsibility for decisions, they often stand alone. These decisions include ways and means to finance the expansion of existing programs and the development of new programs now thrust upon the university. Our presidents must become financial leaders as well as leaders in the more traditional academic sense if they are to meet this challenge.

The establishment of viable systems of governance for our institutions of higher education can no longer remain a matter for scholarly debate. There is a wide range of questions which academic leaders must answer today. They understand the magnitude of the national commitment to higher education. However, lack of precedents and open-ended responsibility often leave these leaders uncertain and frustrated. As they seek to meet the demands of students, faculty, trustees, parents, alumni, and other users of higher education, our top college and university administrators need a new concept of administration which Clark Kerr, James Perkins, Harold W. Dodds,[7] and others have been seeking to define when they have had an opportunity to express themselves on the problem of administering a college or university under present conditions. One aspect of this new concept of academic administration is to augment the pool of identifiable and experienced personnel in positions at or below the level of the dean and in the many other supporting areas necessary for the sound administration of an educational corporation. Another aspect is to clarify the role of an academic administrator today.

1. "Institute for Science and Technology; A Proposal." (New York: April, 1966) (Mimeographed), p. 1.

2. *A Master Plan for Higher Education in California*, 1960-1975 (Sacramento, California: California State Department of Education, 1960), p. 46.

3. Conrad Hilberry, *Growing New Leaders*. An address given at the 1967 meeting of the Association for Higher Education, Chicago, Illinois.

4. Fred M. Hechinger, "Colleges Unsure of Student Role," *The New York Times*, March 16, 1966.

5. Humphrey Doermann, "Financing Higher Education," *Saturday Review* (November 20, 1965), p. 80.

6. See Harry Williams, "Planning for Effective Resource Allocation in Universities," prepared for the Commission on Administrative Affairs of the American Council on Education (Washington, D. C.: American Council on Education, 1966).

7. Clark Kerr, *The Uses of the University* (Cambridge, Mass.: Harvard University Press, 1963); James A. Perkins, *The University in Transition* (Princeton, N. J.: Princeton University Press, 1966); Harold W. Dodds, *The Academic President — Educator or Caretaker?* (New York, N. Y.: McGraw-Hill Book Company, Inc., 1962).

II

The Program of Internships In Academic Administration

The Ellis L. Phillips Foundation's Program of Internships in Academic Administration provided carefully selected individuals with up to a year's leave of absence for self-improvement. It gave them access to a "laboratory," the host institution, and to "directors of research," the mentor at the host college or university, his colleagues, and the foundation's Program Committee.

The aims of the program were to identify persons of promise for administrative work in higher education, to improve their knowledge and skills in the science and art of academic administration, and through them to call attention to the cause of good administration in higher education. The interns observed college and university administration at a decision-making level and they also had an opportunity to study the discipline through an administrative sabbatical and conferences with their colleagues in the program.

The origin and development of the Phillips Internship Program is also an example of how a small foundation can develop a distinctive program of its own. In January of 1959, when Ellis L. Phillips died, his immediate family assumed the responsibility of reorganizing the foundation which he had founded in 1930 and had actively led and supported from 1946 to the time of his death.

In 1959 the foundation had assets of slightly over $2,500,000. The income from this capital would not be sufficient to support a large project, but with an allocation of $40,000 to $50,000 of income, something useful and distinctive could be undertaken. A project in the area of education seemed appropriate. The foundation had a long record of support for education under the leadership of Ellis L. Phillips, particularly in making funds available for buildings to house the School of Electrical Engineering at Cornell University and the Departments of Philosophy, History, Education, and Religion at Ohio

9

Wesleyan University in Delaware, Ohio. Also, the foundation had been the original sponsor of the Commission on the Education of Women, a project of the American Council on Education.

Early in 1961, the President of the Ellis L. Phillips Foundation was authorized to consult with Mrs. Esther Raushenbush, then Dean (and later President) of Sarah Lawrence College. Out of this discussion emerged a plan to select persons on the basis of their potential for academic leadership and to then give them an opportunity to spend up to a year in association with college presidents or other senior officers in order to determine for themselves whether to take the plunge. The premise was that college or university administration can be regarded as an independent profession, like teaching, medicine, and law, rather than merely something one does and is expected to know how to do without training. If the premise were correct, some regard might usefully be given to the problem of identifying good candidates and giving them a period of specialized experience in academic administration.

A Program of Internships in Academic Administration was accordingly authorized. Dr. Arthur S. Adams agreed to serve on an advisory committee for the new program under Esther Raushenbush's chairmanship, and Frederick de Wolfe Bolman, Jr., then President of Franklin and Marshall College in Lancaster, Pennsylvania, was invited to be the third member of the Program Committee.[1] By October, the Program Committee had completed a printed brochure announcing the internship program and had mailed it to approximately 200 college presidents, deans, or other individuals known to the Committee, asking for the names of possible candidates for the internship experience, which would begin in the 1962-63 academic year. A press release was prepared and sent out announcing the program. This appeared in the *New York Herald Tribune* on October 8, 1961, and resulted in several letters of inquiry from individuals.

The response to the mailing was immediate and positive. By November 15th, 68 nominations of possible intern candidates had been received, as well as a number of inquiries asking for information about the program. Eighty-one colleges and universities had by that time indicated a willingness to be host institutions. The foundation sent out letters to the first 68 nominees, along with application blanks for those interested in being considered as candidates. The Program Committee expected to have a comprehensive dossier on each candidate by the end of the year. Each member of the Committee would then read the dossiers and interns would be selected at a Committee meeting following the intensive screening of applications.

When the deadline for applications was reached in the fall of 1961, there had been 78 nominations for the projected four internships, and 85 colleges and universities had indicated a willingness to be hosts to the successful interns. By that time, the foundation had received 136 letters from college presidents and deans commenting on the internship program. There was general agreement that its purposes were worthwhile. There were a number of suggestions about administering the program, and some discussion of parallel programs which either had been instituted or were under consideration. This dialogue, which began with the initial mailing, continued until the conclusion of the program in the spring of 1966 and was extremely useful to those concerned with administering the program.

The annual income of the Ellis L. Phillips Foundation at this time was about $60,000. After modest honoraria for the members of the Program Committee and provision for salaries and fringe benefits of interns on leave, and travel costs, there was no room in the budget for a Director. As a result the Program Committee agreed to oversee the program on a part-time basis.

Early in 1962, Miss Elizabeth Paschal, representative of the Ford Foundation's Fund for the Advancement of Education, expressed interest in the program to Mrs. Raushenbush and Dr. Bolman, and indicated that the Fund might wish to participate financially. Mrs. Raushenbush responded by presenting an informal budget of $140,000 for the academic year 1962-63, this amount to be shared equally by the Fund and the Ellis L. Phillips Foundation. This expanded budget provided for eight internships and included provision for a full-time Program Director. On March 19, Miss Paschal wrote to the Phillips Foundation on behalf of the Fund for the Advancement of Education granting $70,000 to support the internship program, and the Phillips Foundation agreed to increase its commitment to provide the full $140,000 program for 1962-63.

In April, Harry J. Carman, who had retired some years before as Dean of Columbia College, agreed to become Director of the program.[2] Thereafter, the pace of preparation for the initial internship year stepped up. Plans were completed for an opening conference at the Princeton Inn on the weekend of August 31, to which the six men who had accepted internships for the coming academic year were invited together with their mentors from host institutions, and members of the Program Committee. No sooner had the six interns reported to their host institutions than the cycle of the program for the 1963-64 academic year began with a rush. On October 1st, Dr. Carman sent a letter to 250 college and university officials and friends requesting nominations. The Fund for the Advancement of

Education was kept informed of developments and made a second grant of $100,000 to the program. The Ellis L. Phillips Foundation increased its support accordingly, permitting expansion of the program to provide experience for thirteen interns. The program continued at about this level of activity in the 1964-66 academic years, with financial support from the Ellis L. Phillips and Edward W. Hazen Foundations.

The response from the academic community to the internship program bears out the sponsors' premise that new steps are required to seek out and attract men and women who are willing to give their primary attention to the welfare of the academic enterprise rather than to a field of learning. A search for persons with leadership potential and their subsequent direction as interns must be conducted with great care; otherwise, there is a good chance that harm rather than benefit will result to candidates and academic employers alike. The Phillips program was necessarily small and could therefore be conducted on a personal basis. Nominations for interns were solicited by members of the Program Committee on a personal basis and the directors of the program came to know the participants, and often their families, as friends and colleagues with whom they were sharing an educational experience.

The original brochure stated, "The Foundation is especially interested in individuals who might become undergraduate deans or other senior academic officers in liberal arts colleges or universities." This was later broadened to include persons with a possible interest in the wide variety of areas of administrative service which are becoming increasingly important as our educational institutions grow in size and complexity. All officers of college and university administration find satisfaction in a fundamental interest in and loyalty to their academic institution, what it stands for and what it proposes to do. Of course, special skills are required for different positions. This is true for the Academic Dean as well as the Director of Admissions, the Vice President for Business and Finance, Personnel Officer, or Director of Research. However, it is no longer relevant to the needs of the great educational institutions to suggest that only a person with teaching credentials and background is a "line officer." Academic deans, business officers, financial officers and other officers of administration contribute to the processes of higher education, not only with their technical skill but also with their ability to understand, support, and integrate the mission of the college or university in teaching and research.

Therefore, looking beyond the academic deanship, the brochure for the Internship Program explained:

A candidate might be an individual who has given no particular thought to academic administration, but who through committee work and other activities has shown talent for it and could use well the opportunity to explore the possibility of such a career. He might now be holding an administrative post either in business or in a college, or he might wish to move from teaching into college administration.

A well qualified candidate should be a person of excellent character with a broad balanced education, preferably, though not exclusively, in the liberal arts and sciences. Although advanced degrees and teaching experience are valuable assets in this program, they are not requisites.

Although there is no formal ruling or statement as to who shall or shall not be nominated, in establishing its program, its founders had in mind helping young men and women of great future promise to discover their talent for academic administration and to assist those on the lower rounds of the administrative ladder in becoming more effective administrators. Although nominees would be below the rank of full dean, the Program Committee hopes that persons of scholarly promise who have already made a contribution in the realm of scholarship will not be overlooked.

One way to understand the thinking behind the identification and selection of the interns is to look at the record of the 44 men and women who were selected and who accepted internships during the four-year period. From among the 476 men and women nominated for the program, 292 said they would like to be considered and 86 were interviewed by the Directors and Program Committee after their dossiers had been read.

In the 1962-63 academic year the six men selected were experienced teachers. Several had some administrative experience, as an assistant dean in a college of liberal arts, as a director of an extension service, and as a chairman of a university department. All were selected from within the academic community. Their ages ranged from 30 to 40.

In terms of academic disciplines, one of the 1962-63 Phillips interns was from geology, one from political science, two from geography, and two from the behavioral sciences. It seems to be easier to attract persons with backgrounds in the newer academic disciplines into academic administration. Those who have their degrees in classics, English, history, philosophy, and other more traditional liberal arts subjects may prefer to remain in teaching or research. However, in subsequent years there were some interns from these older disciplines. All of the initial interns had earned doctoral degrees. The Program Committee recognized that although academic degrees do not guarantee good performance, weight is given in the academic community to these outward symbols, and the interns with the best possible academic credentials would be likely to get the most out of the experience. The Committee did not make any particular academic degree a condition for the award.

The thirteen interns selected for the following year, 1963-64, were more varied in background. They included three women: a working housewife in Washington, D. C., another who was Assistant Director for Program Development at CARE, Inc., in New York City, and an instructor in social science at a state college. A Marine colonel, formerly Director of Plans and Coordination, Legislative Affairs, Office of the Secretary of Defense, was also selected, as was another man whose experience was primarily in the area of university funds development. The Committee also selected an Assistant Professor of Management in a college of business administration. A majority of the 1963-64 interns came to the program with considerable teaching experience and related academic credentials.

From 1964 to 1966, the program provided experience for twenty-five additional interns from a variety of backgrounds. There was another retired Marine colonel, the Dean of a predominantly Negro college in Alabama, an Assistant Professor of Romance Languages, men with backgrounds in religion and philosophy, a political scientist who was interested in the dynamics of academic government as well as in the possibility of a career in administration, an Assistant Dean of Students, and a man with experience in university fund raising.

Despite differences in background, academic discipline, and employment, their opportunities for taking advantage of the experience tended to be similar once the interns were at their host institutions, and when they assembled at the opening and concluding conferences and at other times during the internship year, the differences of background were blotted out by their common experience and the groups melded together very well. The majority of nominations in the program came from college and university presidents and chancellors. Deans made up the second largest group of nominators, with professors next, vice presidents fourth, and associate and assistant deans fifth. However, names of interesting nominees came from a wide variety of other sources including provosts, vice provosts, and other administrative officers. Good recommendations came from the College Entrance Examination Board, the Cooperative Field Service Program, the Independent College Funds of America, the Director of the Study of American Education, the Institute of Higher Education, the Association of American Colleges, and from a director of college and university assistance of the U.S. Office of Education.

In matching the intern to the host institution, factors considered were each intern's wishes, if expressed, and the opinion of the Program Committee as to what was best for the intern. An effort was made to provide experience in a different part of the country and in a different type of academic setting from the intern's home institution. For example, a Professor of English at Northern Illinois University split his internship between Stanford University and the University of Michigan.

Sometimes the geographical transition was extreme. For instance, one intern came from a position of responsibility for business affairs in the graduate division of the University of California, Berkeley, to spend a year at Dartmouth College. In other cases, there was less change in location. A Texas intern found it desirable for personal reasons to remain in her home state and spend her internship year at the Universities of Houston and Texas. A Director of Community Services at Foothill Junior College in Los Altos, California, was interested in public higher education in California. Since his sponsor wanted him to have experience at the highest level in that system, he was assigned to the University of California, Berkeley. A complete list of "home" and "host" institutions is presented in the Appendix.

The Program Committee sought the same careful matching of mentors at the host institutions for each of the 44 interns. In most instances, the person asked to serve as mentor was known personally by one of the members of the Program Committee or the Director. An effort was made to explain to the mentor what might be required, but this proved to be difficult in practice because each host institution is a unique "academic laboratory" and each mentor a unique "laboratory adviser." In some cases, the mentor took keen personal interest in the intern and gave a great deal of his time to providing a rich and varied experience. Other mentors were either too busy to give much time to the intern or so tied up with other business that, in effect, the intern was left to sink or swim. In some instances, sub-assignments of mentors were arranged by the foundation or were achieved by negotiation on the spot.

The selection of the right person for the internship experience proved to be the key element in the program. A person who has the knowledge, vision, and determination to be a good administrator will be able to provide himself with a first-class educational experience as an intern at a wide variety of institutions, whether or not his mentor is able to help him. On the other hand, a poorly qualified intern will probably get little out of the experience, even if his mentor is able to provide time and opportunity for his guidance and entry into the full range of activity at the host institution.

Many of the mentors were presidents of colleges or universities, some were deans, and some were academic officers with quite different responsibilities. The value of the experience depended on personal factors and the administrative climate of the host institution, not on the title of the mentor. From the mentor's point of view, the relationship with his intern varied considerably, but it cannot be doubted that the program had an impact on mentor and host institution. One mentor summed up the relationship as follows:

What is the most effective relationship for an intern to his mentor and to the host institution: Assistant to the President or other administrative officer; specific tasks of administrative responsibility; study of specific problems as a general student of administration or as a participant-observer with the mentor in the various tasks of administration? I'm sure that we could use one or all of these in the course of a year of an intern's experience. And I'm not sure that there is any one which is superior to another. . . .

Perhaps the most important part of the mentor's role is interpretation, answering the inevitable question — WHY? Now it's true that the administrator-mentor may not really know why, but his function is to interpret to the extent of his knowledge and understanding the situations which have, for some reason or other, excited the fancy of the intern.

And here I think I get to the most rewarding part of the internship experience for the mentor. In trying to explain and interpret for an inquisitive intern, the mentor will learn an unbelievable amount about himself, his colleagues, and his own institution. . . .

Now a final point. Administrative capacity consists of two parts, as I see it. The knowledge and skill of how to do it and second, an attitude of respect and sympathetic understanding toward people for whom the administration is carried on. Along with the observation of the administrative process, the interns will absorb the attitudes and emotional reactions of the administrators to their jobs and to their people. Obviously, proper attitudes, tons of good will, will have little administrative value in the absence of knowledge and skill. But, similarly, the most extensive knowledge and the most refined skills are worthless unless there is a deep respect and genuine interest in students, faculty, staff and other associates.

Now, how this emotional aspect of administrative development can be woven into the internship I don't know. This is one of the big areas that we know very little about. . . . I think that this area of developing emotional capacity for administration, particularly in the educational field, is one of the areas that desperately needs exploration by people who are sensitive to this particular aspect of administration.

It is not too difficult to understand the impact of the internship on the mentor and host institution, ranging from some inconvenience, extra expense, and, at times, irritation, to a genuine sense of interest in and benefit from having the intern on the premises asking questions and perhaps helping out on projects. In several instances, the interns served as assistants to presidents or vice presidents or other officers and performed services for the host institution. However, the value of the intern to the host institution was always incidental to his role as student and observer of the art of administration.

More subtle and difficult to assess is the qualitative impact of the program on the intern himself and on his understanding of the processes of administration. One intern summarized his year's experience in a letter to the Director:

This year has given me the opportunity to study the structure and functioning of an entire university from a vantage point few faculty ever have. The tangible result of this experience is that I am much more knowledgeable in and sensitive to the problems and complexities of higher education and its institutions. But more important than this, the year has afforded me the chance to observe the people who guide the destinies of an educational institution. Their philosophies of higher education, their abilities to resolve complex problems — deciding what to do and then how and when, their concerns for the professional and social well-being of their constituents, their computer-like storehouse of facts and figures on their institution and its people, their abilities to successfully juggle a dozen balls in the air at one time, their sense and use of the history and evolution of the institution that they lead; all these intangibles of the makeup of a top administrator have rubbed off on me this year, and I like to think I'm the better for it.

Another intern in his more detailed report to the Program Committee wrote of sitting in on a wide variety of conferences involving his mentor (academic dean of a large private university) and savoring "the full panoply of idiosyncrasies denoted by the terms 'faculty member' or 'fellow administrator'." The intern was invited to join the budget struggle as one of the dean's analysts and he ran studies ranging from the average size of sections in all beginning classes offered by the college to library book purchase allocations and the effectiveness of a program of intramural athletics. After noting many other brushes with the real world of academic administration, both on campus and at deans' meetings he attended with his mentor, this

intern described the influences on his attitude toward administration
which he found most significant:

The internship has inclined me to the view that the "structure" or "pattern"
of administration is not so important as are the individuals involved. I believe I really was naive enough to assume one might evolve a neat,
"legalistic" scheme in which the "powers" or areas of responsibility were
"correctly ordered." Members of the faculty, department chairmen, deans,
provosts, financial officers, boards of governors — all would have their scope
clearly delineated and nicely balanced. That is of course utter nonsense.

The truth of the matter is that almost all policy decisions involve all
"partners" so completely that few of these decisions, if any, can properly be
entrusted to any one or two. What one wants is administrators capable of
creating an atmosphere in which an honest effort will be made to solve a
problem by all interested parties.

This can perhaps best be seen if one considers what is popularly termed
the "role of the faculty." How can it be described? What "ought" it to be?
Despite the siren call of the "professional administrator," I would insist that
it has to be one of fundamental importance in decision making. If the function of a university - its "business" - is the advancement and transmission
of knowledge, what policy relevant to that "business" does not impinge
upon a faculty's areas of competence?

Of course, it is true that some faculty members are greedy, or selfish, or
spoiled, or impractical, or stubborn. Still, they remain the priceless and indispensable ingredient. The art (which I believe is a more accurate descrip-
tive term than "science") of administration lies in being able to bring the not
inconsiderable talents of the faculty to bear upon administrative problems in
constructive ways, not to hedge them off. . . .

What we are really talking about is some skill in interpersonal relations, and
so we are concerned with the talents of an individual (or individuals), not
the efficacy of a governing structure.

The internship in academic administration offers exposure to the
art of administration in company with practitioners of that art. This
is probably its most valuable feature as a device for offering some
degree of training and exciting interest in academic administration as
a career.

1. In the summer of 1964, two additional members were invited to join the Program
   Committee and accepted: Robert W. Merry of the Graduate School of Business
   Administration, Harvard University, and Robert J. Wert, formerly of Stanford
   University, now President of Mills College.

2. Dean Carman was one of the most "unretired" men in American higher education.
   Despite many other active interests, he devoted a great deal of time and energy to
   the Phillips Internship Program until his death in December 1964.

III

Education In Academic Administration

The Program of Internships in Academic Administration was sponsored by the Ellis L. Phillips Foundation not as a part of any local, regional, or national plan to increase the supply of able administrators in higher education; the program evolved from observations and ideas of the Program Committee and the foundation's Board of Directors. They were engaging in the old-fashioned American exercise of taking initiative to meet a need, rather than responding to an external plan. As the program developed, an attempt was made to determine the relationship between the Phillips Internship Program and other efforts to identify and provide experience for potential leaders in academic administration.

Information about other programs was collected. Letters of inquiry were sent to likely sources. The foundation became a modest clearing-house for information on programs in the United States that were concerned with more effective administration in higher education.[1]

FORMAL INSTRUCTION

One way to identify and train administrators in higher education is to develop special academic programs in administration that lead toward a graduate degree. A number of teachers' colleges have long had such programs for primary and secondary school administrators, but there is no similar tradition for the university level. During the Phillips Program, there were lively panel discussions on whether academic administration in higher education is a discipline which lends itself to systematic study, or whether it is an art, something to which one brings innate ability and in which one becomes competent through trial by battle. However, even if one accepts the concept of

19

administration as a discipline there is little if any opposition in the academic community to the concept of formal education for administrative positions in colleges and universities.

Some programs do offer degrees in higher education. One is at Syracuse University where both doctors' and masters' degrees may be obtained, and where a work-study graduate program in student personnel is also in progress. Professor E. D. Duryea, Chairman of the Program in Higher Education, reported in 1965, that he had several majors who were planning careers in various phases of general administration. This included: finance, business affairs, admissions, registration, public relations, fund raising, institutional research, and alumni relations. Other candidates hoped to qualify for academic posts as assistants to deans or presidents. He reported that some degree candidates at the School of Education planned to enter academic administration in the two-year college field.

Indiana University offers an interdisciplinary doctoral program in its Department of Higher Education. Between the inception of the department in 1958 and 1967 over 100 men and women had graduated, eight to become college or university presidents and others to assume teaching positions, deanships, and various administrative assignments at colleges and universities in the United States and abroad. The School of Education at Stanford University has a graduate degree program under the direction of Lewis B. Mayhew, Professor of Education, for persons desiring to enter administrative posts in higher education. In November, 1964, Teachers College of Columbia University inaugurated a Department of Higher Education, supplementing the College's Institute of Higher Education. The department seeks to attract mature persons for post-doctoral instruction including administration, and its program offers an opportunity for practical experience in administration in conjunction with course work.

The W. K. Kellogg Foundation has assisted many persons preparing themselves for administration in junior colleges by its funding of Junior College Leadership Centers in different parts of the United States. Fellowships are available to candidates for the doctor of education or the doctor of philosophy degrees with a specialization in junior college administration, who qualify for matriculation in the graduate school of the host university. The Kellogg Program is pointing the way toward meeting the great demand for administrative leadership in the rapidly growing field of junior or intermediate college education in the United States. The School of General Studies at Columbia University, beginning with the 1963-64 academic year, has awarded more than sixty New Career Fellowships to persons who wish to enter a "service" career after a career in business. Financial assistance has been provided by a grant from the Ford Foundation. Applicants must have held responsible posts during the course of their business or professional careers and be between thirty-five and fifty years of age. Successful candidates received fellowships covering tuition fees for full-time course work in an undergraduate or graduate division of Columbia University. Several of the participants have entered academic administration. Funding of the New Career Program after 1969 is uncertain.

Since the mid-1950's, the School of Education at the University of Michigan has offered doctoral and post-doctoral courses at its Center for the Study of Higher Education. The faculty of the Michigan Department of Higher Education includes men with degrees in engineering, law, business administration, psychology, and political science, in addition to those who have the traditional education degrees. The founder and until recently Director of the Center is Professor Algo Henderson, now Research Professor at the Center for Research and Development in Higher Education at the University of California, Berkeley. Professor Henderson, Professor T. R. McConnell of the University of California's Center, and Professor W. H. Cowley of Stanford are pioneers in the relatively new approach to a systematic study of higher education as an academic discipline.

There are a number of other opportunities for course work in administration in higher education. One example is the program of the College Personnel Institute, Claremont, California. There, candidates for positions as deans of students may study for M.A. and Ph.D. degrees in the Claremont Graduate School and University Center. This program may set a pattern for advanced degree work in other specialties in higher education—in business, or personnel administration, for example. It is an open question whether entry into the profession of academic administration will continue to be overwhelmingly from the traditional academic disciplines, perhaps coupled with an internship or other special training, or whether there will be greater use of the route of the master's or doctor's degree in a discipline of higher education. Meanwhile, the centers for the study of higher education perform an undoubted service to the profession by providing a systematic study of academic administration in our colleges and universities.

INTERNSHIPS

The internship is another method of identifying future academic leaders. At the college and university levels it is essentially a period of self-directed study. The intern is engaged in research in higher education and the host institution which has accepted him for the period of leave is his laboratory. The mentor who is responsible for guiding and assisting the intern at the host institution, and the Program Committee, and Director, if the program has outside sponsorship, are the intern's laboratory consultants.

An administrative training project with substantial college and university budget support is the Leadership Training Project (now the Consultant-Examiner Associate Program) of the North Central Association of Colleges and Secondary Schools. This program, initiated in 1957 with support from the Carnegie Corporation, selects between twenty and forty Consultant-Examiner Associates annually from the faculty and the administrative staffs of association members. Each associate undergoes a year's orientation during which he may visit member institutions and work with officers of administration, in addition to attending conferences and doing supervised study.

The project's immediate goal is to prepare people to serve as accrediting examiners and consultants for the Association. A long-range result has been to develop future academic leaders for members and thus for American higher education. As early as 1961 the Executive Secretary of the project, Norman Burns, reported in a letter to the foundation that although so select a group would be destined for success in any case, the program has helped not only in the education of the participants but in adding to their visibility. A number of the younger participants have moved into positions of higher responsibility, one as president of a college, others in vice-presidencies and deanships.

The idea of the internship for a potential executive is neither new nor limited to the traditional academic community. In 1949 the Navy Department was one of a group of federal agencies which sponsored the first management internships in the federal government. The University of Chicago has developed a fellowship-internship program in continuing education with the support of the W. K. Kellogg Foundation. Those who win the awards become acquainted not only with the theoretical foundations of adult education, but also with the practical problems encountered in the day-to-day operation of a university-based adult education center.

The internship experience does not consist entirely of observation, self-directed "laboratory" work at the host institution, and self-directed study. The Phillips Internship Program encouraged systematic study of higher education and the problems of academic administration at opening and closing conferences, through distribution of a reading list and through personal contact and correspondence with members of the Program Committee. In 1964 the Ford Foundation granted $4,750,000 to the American Council on Education, Washington, D. C., to plan and put into operation its Internship Program for Fellows in Academic Administration. This program includes opening and closing seminars of several days' duration, at which the participants are introduced to much of the formal material relating to higher education as an academic discipline.[2]

The American Council and Phillips interns were asked to prepare written reports on the philosophy and operation of the host institutions and on topics of a more general nature relating to administration. However, self-directed reading, discussion with fellow interns and host colleagues, and opportunities to pursue questions of special interest are probably of great value in the experience. To cite two examples of self-directed study done by Phillips interns: One spent ten days at the U.S. Office of Education in Washington and at public and private agencies there, acquainting himself with the sources of the literature on higher education which flows out of our capital city. His report on this experience was an *aide-memoire* for himself and a document of interest to his colleagues. Another was interested in the Conant Plan for improving teacher education in the liberal arts; with the cooperation of the Director, he corresponded with the key officer for the Conant experiment at each of the cooperating New York colleges and followed up this correspondence with on-site visits, where appropriate.[3]

SHORTER PROGRAMS FOR WORKING ADMINISTRATORS

There are a number of conferences, workshops, and work-study sessions for college and university administrators. One of the most interesting is the Institute for College and University Administrators founded in 1955 and supported with generous grants from the Carnegie Corporation and, more recently, from the Danforth Foundation. The Institute invites recently appointed college and university presidents to come together for ten days in the summer and, since 1958, has offered somewhat shorter winter institutes for deans. At the institutes the participants discuss written descriptions of problems faced by college and university administrators, these case studies being supplemented by the contributions of authorities in the field. Separate sessions are held for the wives of the presidents. Presumably the deans' wives have been too busy to attend. The Institute was lodged at the Harvard Business School until 1965 and is now associated with the American Council on Education in Washington, D. C. Meetings have been held in a variety of academic settings.

Since 1966 the Institute has scheduled sessions of three days each for trustees and departmental chairmen and five-day sessions for senior academic business officers. An Institute for Deans of Schools of Engineering has been sponsored for the last several years by the Engineering College Administrative Council of the American Society for Engineering Education.

Summer workshops for administrators with various specialties or for persons in administration have been sponsored at many schools of education, including New York and Stanford Universities, the Municipal University of Omaha, and the University of California, Berkeley. The University of Michigan has a program of "after hours" management development seminars open to officers of administration.

Many of the specialists in academic administration look to the relatively short but intensive workshop or institute as a means of professional upgrading. For example, the National Association of Educational Buyers sponsors three- or four-day annual institutes on the professional growth of college business personnel. At the institutes, there is an opportunity to consider a wide range of questions concerning higher education and the administration of colleges and universities. Other administrative specialties sponsor short training programs which, while they deal more with bread-and-butter aspects of administration, are increasingly concerned with the broad problems faced by colleges and universities today. Examples are the workshop which the Eastern Association of College and University Business Officers conducts every other year, and the workshop for incoming development officers sponsored by the American College Public Relations Association.

In 1967, the president of the Eastern Association of College and University Business Officers appointed a Committee on Professional Development which submitted a report dealing with the role of academic administrators today, procedures to attract persons to service in administration, and programs for professional improvement at various career levels. The Board of Directors of the National Association of College and University Business Officers has recently established a permanent Committee of Professional Development.

The College Student Personnel Institute is seeking funds to support a professional development program which will include four-week summer sessions and a session of one to four weeks during the academic year. The program will provide a participating "fellow" an opportunity to concentrate on specific problems or issues of importance on his home campus and to devote himself to broader theoretical or philosophial considerations in college student personnel work.

The Junior College Leadership Centers, described earlier, offer in-service conferences and workshops for administrators. Summer conferences, institutes, or workshops for officers of administration can provide intellectual stimulation and an opportunity for administrators to meet and discuss their problems in a relaxed atmosphere away from the tyranny of in- and out-baskets. An example is the Pugwash Intellectual Life Conferences, week-long seminars sponsored in the 1950's by the Association of American Colleges with financial support from the Carnegie Corporation and Cyrus Eaton. The Association of American Colleges recently considered and sought financing for a "time-off-for-presidents" program which would be modeled on the Pugwash Experiment.

EFFORTS TO PROVIDE TIME AND OPPORTUNITY FOR SELF-IMPROVEMENT

If a one-week summer conference can benefit a college president or dean or even a tired college business officer, certainly a longer period of leave would also beneft him and thus the institution he serves. However, it has not been customary for educational corporations to offer officers of administraton the sabbatical, half-year leave with full pay or full year with half pay, often offered to faculty at appropriate career intervals. The internship programs, as noted earlier, do offer a degree of freedom to the participants to develop and pursue their own lines of intellectual inquiry.

One of the most interesting time-off plans was the Carnegie Corporation's Academic Administrators' Grants. Beginning with the 1939-40 academic year, the presidents of several institutions were asked to keep an eye out for young administrators of promise and to release such officers for a period of two to four months so that they could make leisurely visits to colleges and universities in other parts of the country for observation and study. Several of the early grantees have become presidents of leading universities or otherwise distinguished themselves in academic administration. From 1948 to 1966 the Carnegie Corporation awarded ninety-three travel grants.

The Carnegie Corporation still provides a refreshment time-off and travel program for college and university presidents, a trip of two or three months outside the United States. About three recipients are selected each year.

THE STUDY OF HIGHER EDUCATION AND THE THEORY OF ACADEMIC ADMINISTRATION

A primary function of the centers or institutes described earlier is the systematic study of higher education, including the theory of administration. As administration in higher education gains recognition as a graduate discipline, course work and research in the subject matter will receive greater intellectual and financial support from the various university graduate departments or schools. The Center for the Study of Higher Education at the University of Michigan, for example, may become a distinct graduate department outside the School of Education. Such recognition, however, must be earned in competition with the many other graduate disciplines which draw upon the university budget. Up to now, much of the financial support for the study of college and university administration has come from outside sources.

A primary emphasis at the Center for Research and Development in Higher Education at the University of California, Berkeley, and at the Institute of Higher Education, Teachers College, Columbia University, has been on continuing research in subjects relating to administration in higher education. Some of the California research projects have received government support money. The Carnegie Corporation has given a total of some $800,000 to the Teachers College Institute to study professional schools and liberal arts colleges. The staff of the Berkeley Center includes a number of research psychologists and sociologists; the faculty advisory committee has included representatives of the departments of English, philosophy, physics, and political science.

Algo Henderson has suggested that more scholarly research should be done in the history and philosophy of higher education and in the theory of organization, of administrative behavior, of administrative procedure, and of decision-making. He notes that much is known about the decision-making process in relation to public administration and business administration, but that much more study is required before this knowledge can be applied to the governance of colleges and universities. He mentions in this connection the contribution of Robert W. Merry at the Harvard Business School and of other social scientists at Michigan and elsewhere who are examining group participation as a basis for a theory of organization and administration in higher education.[4]

The Junior College Leadership Centers sponsored by the Kellogg Foundation also engage in research programs relating to junior college administration; research has also been carried out through *ad hoc* study groups. One such group is the New York State Regents Advisory Committee on Educational Leadership, which under the chairmanship of President James A. Perkins of Cornell University and the direction of Dean F. H. Stutz of the Cornell School of Education, and John K. Hemphill of the Educational Testing Service, studied all levels of educational administration in the State of New York.[5] Another study, directed by Professor Francis E. Rourke of the Department of Political Science at The Johns Hopkins University, examined managerial innovations at selected state universities across the country.[6] Both of these studies were made possible by the generosity of the Carnegie Corporation.

Improvement in recruiting and training officers of administration is not a fringe benefit. It is a condition of the future excellence of our colleges and universities. Not enough is being done at a time when colleges and universities are growing rapidly in size and complexity. A few degree programs in schools of education; one or two centers for the study of and research in higher education which have to fight hard for financial support; scattered programs of internships in academic administration and shorter institutes or workshops for some groups of working administrators; a few time-off opportunities — these steps do not add up to sufficient progress toward more effective administration in higher education.

1. Information collected through Spring, 1966 is reported in an article by the author, "Toward More Effective Administration in Higher Education," *The Educational Record,* XLVII, 2 (Spring 1966) (Washington, D.C.: American Council on Education), pp. 148-162.

2. See Lanier Cox, "The A.C.E. Academic Administration Internship Program" and Alexander W. Astin, "Research Findings on the Academic Administration Internship Program," *The Educational Record* (Spring, 1966), pp. 163-184. More than 100 interns had been appointed A.C.E. Fellows in Academic Administration by the end of the 1967-68 academic year. At that time a sharp reduction in available funds caused a revision in the program. Beginning in 1968-69 the 50 to 60 member colleges and universities which participated in the program appointed and financed their own interns. The Council prepared guidelines for structuring the internship, either at the appointing institution or at a host institution. The Council also offered a study program, staff consultation, and other services. It designated some of the interns as Council Fellows to be invited to opening and closing seminars.

3. See *Report of Final Conference Five College Project: Innovation, Opportunity, Creativity*—Report of the proceedings of the Five-College Project Conference held

in Albany, New York on May 17, 1968: University of the State of New York, Division of Teacher Education and Certification, Albany, N. Y. December, 1968.

4. Raymond F. Howes, (Ed.), *Toward Better Preparation of College and University Administrators* (Washington, D. C.: Association for Higher Education of the National Education Association, 1964), pp. 26-29.

5. Publications of the committee include: *College and University Trustees and Trusteeship* (1966); *College and University Presidents* (1967); and *Leadership for Education* (1967).

6. Glenn E. Brooks and Francis E. Rourke, *The Managerial Revolution in Higher Education* (Baltimore, Md.: The Johns Hopkins Press, 1966).

IV

The Interns Speak Out

The Director of the Phillips Internship Program sent out question-
naires to the forty-four former interns inviting their comments on
the program and their views on questions concerning administration
in higher education. Excerpts from their answers and from interns'
reports which were made either during or at the end of the internship year are included in this chapter. Several reports reflect the
lively debates at the spring and closing conferences, others offer observations and information gained through individual contact.

Almost all the interns entered academic adminstration. Whether
this is because of prior disposition, the effect of the experience,
because of an intern's being marked by his nominators and second-
ers as a potential academic leader, or to other factors is difficult to
determine. Most of the interns, in their replies to the foundation's
questionnaire, agreed with the premise of the Phillips Internship Program that there is a shortage of persons with qualities and aptitudes
for administration in higher education. They encountered poor administrators as well as good administrators in their host institutions.
They observed that there are many candidates for positions in
academic administration, but the problem is to find highly qualified
people for the positions at hand or in prospect. They agreed with the
premise of the program that officers already serving in administrative posts in higher education can benefit from additional in-service
training and experience. However, the internship is not the only way
to do this, and a number of replies to this question made the point
that Centers for the Study of Higher Education (at Berkeley, Columbia, Michigan, Stanford, and elsewhere) serve an extremely useful
purpose in developing and transmitting principles and standards of
academic administration.

Several respondents suggested that within colleges and universities
a scheme could and should be developed to bring likely young
teachers to the attention of the administration by offering experience

as assistants to deans, or in other ways. This would encourage interested teachers to consider administration and give those in positions of responsibility an opportunity to see them at work. There is a model for such a program at Brown University where young faculty members are brought into the administration, relieved of some teaching responsibility, and assigned to each undergraduate class as assistants to the dean. They remain in the administration as counselors to a class throughout its four-year stay at the university. Such persons may return to full-time teaching or may remain in the administration as a result of this experience.

The interns were asked to comment on the nature of academic administration as science or art. Most of those who answered this question agreed that the history of education and principles of organization, and administration are components of a "science" of administration. All agreed that dealing with academic people, hiring and firing, and making and taking responsibility for decisions on the academic life of the institution involve skills which can be learned only by observation augmented by experience. In this sense, the internship is perhaps the only way one can "learn" the art of administration. The interns were asked to consider the relationship between academic administration and non-academic administration and whether their internship experiences had affected their understanding of the varieties of administrative service in a college or university. Their answers suggest that they learned how complex colleges and universities have become. They became aware of the importance of budget procedure in academic policy. They learned that a good parking program may be important in the smooth running of an institution, even though several steps removed from teaching, research, and the usual orbit of student interest. Many interns sat with the highest councils, including the trustees and appropriations committees of state legislatures, and learned that a college president is deeply concerned with the source of funds for his institution, even if the faculty and student body are relatively unconcerned with such matters.

The interns gained a healthy respect for the various specialties in academic administration. Many of them noted that the highest academic credentials are useful and desirable for the academic deanship and presidency but they also reported the desirability of selecting as business officers, personnel officers, development officers, admissions officers, and others, often classified as "non-academic" administrators, persons with a deep interest in and understanding of the academic process.

The internship experience contributed to each intern's theory of the governance of a college and university and the relationship of students, faculty, administration, trustees, and others to the balance of power in college and university affairs. All of the interns had an opportunity to read extensively in the literature of higher education and to discuss the subject with colleagues. They had time to think about trends in higher education and to note how these trends were affecting their home and host institutions. They attended the opening and closing conferences of the Phillips Internship Program where current questions of interest to academic administrators were discussed and debated. They corresponded with their colleagues, with the Program Committee, and with the Director. They attended annual meetings of the Association for Higher Education and other organizations at which administrative theory and the practical aspects of running colleges and universities are considered. The answers to the Director's questionnaire suggest that their perspective on higher education was broadened and deepened by the internship experience.

The financial aspects of administration in higher education, often not in the ken of a faculty member, were brought sharply to the interns' attention. One intern was told by his mentor that really knowing how the budget is put together, the rationale of the financial reports, how money is sought from the legislature, and why, is the most important thing to be learned by an aspirant for high academic office. Following are some of the interns' comments on this and other major topics of concern.

The Relationship of Teacher, Scholar, and Administrator

I must admit a certain skepticism about a career in academic administration, yet I had long been a fascinated observer of the social process as it occurs on the campus. One reason for hesitancy in seeking a post in administration was my satisfaction with the role of teacher and reseacher. When I viewed the possible rewards of administrative duties in comparison with those of the professor, there seemed little incentive to join the ranks of administration either from the financial or psychic point of view. Yet there was some bait in the trap which I had set myself, arising from the oft-repeated phrase: "There must be a better way." The internship . . . provided me with the experience and evidence that indeed there was and is a better way.

The university professor turned administrator proceeds to justify his own existence by means of new rationalizations. To his former "output", restricted to thinking, saying and writing, he now adds "doing." He attempts to orient this "doing" toward the ultimate aim of his previous activities, namely, teaching in its highest sense which involves both the acquisition and dissemination of knowledge. . . . by administering an institution of higher learning, or a segment of it, he endeavors to do more for teaching as an administrator than he was ever able to do as a scholar. Like Skinner's pigeons trying to match new responses to familiar stimuli, it is vitally important for him to be rewarded with palpable achievement all the way along his newly chosen path. . . . If I should accept a full-time administrative assignment, I would not pretend to be more than an enlightened *amateur* in my formal field. I would, however, devote my research skills acquired as a scholar to the serious study of what I would consider my "new" subject matter: higher education. Acting in this manner, I would not only hope to remain intellectually alive, but I would also increase my leadership opportunities. Indeed, a very large part of the success of an administrator can be ascribed to his detailed and critical knowledge of his institution and to his ability to articulate the problems of his institution within the context of American higher education in general.

The chief value of an internship is to provide an opportunity for experience without responsibility. The assumption of responsibility is one of the most important adjustments for academic administrators, and especially for those whose previous experience is academic. . . . Service on the firing line soon separates faculty from administrators.

Attracting and Keeping Good People in Academic Administration

I see the primary value in the internship program not in identifying potential administrators . . . but in preparing them properly for the transition from one role to another. I do feel a real shortage of persons with the right *training* in academic administration, and feel that in this realm the internship is extremely valuable.

. . . research in the area of faculty attraction and retention indicates that many of the best people in higher education leave or are "forced out" . . . in the face of poor personnel policies and practices and . . . working conditions. . . . People have yet to come to grips with the fact that this is a personnel problem, and that well-planned programs for identifying, attracting, training and retaining good administrators must be developed at each university or college.

. . . the shortage of competent academic administrators lies in what I consider to be the fact that there are relatively few "normal routes" into administrative posts, and it is generally considered to be poor taste (and even poorer politics) to evidence any interest in administration. Further, departmentalization and the pressure of one's own scholarly discipline make it difficult for the young professor to think beyond his own particular field or department. . . . On an institutional level, the administration can help identify and train future leaders through stimulating faculty participation in the governance of the institution . . . thus fostering the sort of climate which would encourage the faculty to think and act beyond their own department or college. Perhaps one or more key members of significant committees should be given reduced teaching loads and travel funds in order that they might talk and meet with equivalent committees at other institutions.

I would attempt first to heighten the overall image of the field of administration. This could be done a variety of ways: by the granting of sabbaticals to administrators; development of more regional conferences; by continuation of internships . . . and by sheer publicity, within universities and colleges, of the opportunities offered in the administrative field.

I believe higher education to be the poorest run and managed of any major area in our society. While I don't buy the corporate analogy, I do not subscribe to the belief that higher education is so different and sacred that it cannot be managed. Scholarship and freedom of inquiry within the almost non-boundaries of teaching can and should exist within a clean and orderly house which avows good stewardship. . . . Administration, really leadership, needs to be less in quantity and scope, yet better in quality.

Knowing the value of the internships in academic administration and the problem of many universities in the developing countries, it would indeed be of great benefit if some administrators from foreign institutions would be permitted to enjoy the opportunities of an internship on the same basis as those of us who were fortunate enough to be selected. . . . If there is a shortage of potential candidates for academic administration in this country, and I believe that there is, the situation is even more difficult in many universities abroad. Many of the universities are very new and the faculty have been largely trained as research scholars in the United States and some of the other highly developed countries. Many of them have little experience in developing curriculum or providing academic leadership. At the same time, there are no senior administrators in their universities to look to for guidance, for they are pioneers in the development of new educational institutions in new nations.[1]

The Relationship Between the Academic and Non-Academic Administrator

I think the academic community should be indivisible. . . . If a man is an accountant at the university, this is something rather different from being an accountant in a corporation . . . even the modern non-academic administrator, it seems to me, must be conversant with academic objectives and the academic mind, otherwise he may fail in spite of excellent technical qualifications and training.

. . . until I became an intern . . . I just accepted the standard mythology that these [non-academic] jobs were . . . unimportant and the people in them were naturally inferior. Now I feel strongly that the work of top-level administrators would be greatly aided by more adequate logistic support in the areas of housing, student aid, admissions, registration, placement, student activities, parking, security, physical plant, etc.

My internship period has convinced me that although there are many businesslike aspects about academic institutions, it is impossible to administer them as one would administer an industry. This means that you are seeking administrators with business competence, but also with a commitment to higher education and an understanding of academic life. This does not mean that it is impossible to train those outside the academic profession to work inside it as academic administrators. On the contrary, it is often very desirable to do this, since such persons will lack many inhibitions that traditional faculty members may have. However, the training is essential. . .

Governance of Colleges and Universities

I believe that students should participate in rule-making as they do in rule-keeping and in matters of educational affairs.

It was my feeling . . . that . . . the time had come to shift to an administrative pattern which paused and looked at where the institution was . . . it seems to me that the various roles played by the trustees, administration, faculty, and students will change as the institution moves through its life cycle. . . . I had an opportunity to observe a truly large and complex institution. I was interested to see whether or not problems were significantly "different" in such an institution . . . my feeling was that problems may have been different in degree, but not in kind.

Trustees are, I believe, the most obvious dinosaurs of our age . . . no longer should trustees be directly responsible for an enterprise which few of them can understand, and [in] which in order to be good trustees, [they] must delegate everything while still being totally and ultimately responsible . . . I think earlier [before the internship experience] I believed that administrators run universities. They don't. They can't. Now I think they shouldn't. They must, however, lead!

In an institution with a strong faculty, a strong administration is a valuable asset. In an institution with a weak faculty, it is an absolute necessity.

As a college grows, it can no longer remain an ivory tower or a monastery; it becomes more like a city with all the needs and strains and diversities which characterize that sort of community. Viewed in that context, it is no longer possible to say categorically that the faculty are totally responsible for this, the administration for that, or that the students are here simply to be taught. The life of higher education is changing too much and the relationships are too interwoven for that. Additionally, one must keep in mind that the line between "faculty" and "student" is becoming less and less clear as graduate education and scholarly research continue to become more and more central to the aims and objectives of higher education. Timing, too, is important; in today's fast moving world, what may be an "administrative" matter at one time may, as a result of changing relationships within or even outside the institution, become a "faculty" concern later on. Thus, I see a tri-lateral relationship among the students, faculty and administration which must be fashioned and fostered to coincide with the historical and planned developmental path of the college itself. We seem to be in a period of rapid and substantial change in the faculty and student sectors, change which may take the academic community at large in many directions, but at least one thing appears certain: colleges and universities are more actively in the forefront in shaping the life and future of this country. And in this continuing trend, I see the administration's role as one of leadership as well as one of helping to bind together the mutual interests of the faculty and the student body; of striving continually to reconcile the inevitable conflicts which develop between these two groups; of providing the material services to and imposing reasonable controls on both sides; and . . . [relating and interacting] on the community at large as freely as possible.

I reject the notion that the term "academic" includes everything that goes on in a college or university and that the teaching faculty should make all the decisions. Further, it appears that we limit their education by refusing to allow students, especially graduate students who are teaching and research assistants, some voice in governance. And, finally, some matters must be handled only by the administrative officers, and both the faculty and the students must refrain from forcing their will upon the appointed officials.

The Role of the Liberal Arts College

I am convinced that it is a mistake to conduct the education of undergraduates in the large and complex institutions. Undergraduate colleges should be relatively small. Groups of undergraduate colleges, perhaps, may be associated with a large and complex university, but one of the most critical problems of undergraduate education is finding faculty willing to devote themselves to the undergraduate. This leads me to suggest that the basic governmental units of even a large institution ought to be relatively small.

Insofar as the College of Liberal Arts is concerned, as goes it, so goes the university. Professional education within the university, especially in the area of medicine, is becoming a kind of monster which threatens to become the tail wagging the dog. I am somewhat concerned about the amount of support which comes to higher education from sources other than endowments, gifts and state appropriations. The federal government's crusade for accountability is absorbing far too much faculty and administrative time on campuses where federal support plays a significant role.

Courses can be taught liberally within any college in the university, and liberal instruction is not confined to the liberal arts college . . . A knowledge of the topic [curriculum] was lacking in my background, and I was glad to have the opportunity to look at it.

Financing Higher Education in the Face of the Upward Spiral of Costs and Demand for Services

My overall view, acquired during the intern year and re-emphasized since, is that higher education, at a time at least of a crisis in numbers and money, has failed really to "level with the people." It has taken to the media to cry need rather than to disseminate interpretive understanding. The chief reason higher education can't level or get across to the public what it is really about is that higher education itself doesn't know . . . In short, the great measurer refuses on almost any basis to measure itself.

It is obvious with federal and state money and the desire for all types of support that both public and private institutions are heading in the direction of one-third tax support, one-third customer pay, and one-third private fund raising.

I was amazed to discover the extent to which private institutions rely upon public sources of funds. The internship experience impressed upon me the epicentral position of universities in our society. Most other institutions have come to look upon them as reservoirs, not only for the transmission, but for the production of knowledge. . . . Some research—generally referred to as departmental research—is necessary to maintain quality instructional programs, but when faculty begin expending more time on non-instructional than instructional activity, it is time for a reappraisal. One suggestion . . . is . . . the establishment of research institutes, perhaps affiliated with, but yet sufficiently distinct from, a college or university, to permit the faculty and the administration to readily distinguish between what and how much individuals do for each type of organization.

The spiral . . . will continue as long as the American economy continues to expand. Relatively speaking, the larger, well-regarded universities should have less trouble in controlling their financial situations—it is the small, private colleges which face the larger danger.

1. The Ford Foundation in Mexico announced in November, 1966 a one-year non-degree program of U. S. study and internship for young (25-35) Mexican university administrators for both public and private institutions of higher education in Mexico. Advanced study in the field of higher education and close work with senior university administrators in a variety of U. S. institutions of higher learning were included. The U. S. universities supervising the first year of the program were the University of California Center for the Study of Higher Education and the University of Wisconsin, Milwaukee Campus.

V

Proposals to Clarify and Strengthen Academic Administration

There is, and probably will continue to be, a "teacher gap", a shortage of faculty members with good qualifications and ability. However, many steps have been taken by colleges, universities, foundations, and government to meet this need. Also, we may anticipate an adequate supply of well qualified men and women for top administrative positions, although at the junior college level and at some of the smaller colleges there will be a problem. The internship programs point up the critical manpower need facing our colleges and universities. We need persons with a new standard of excellence to fill the middle ranks of academic administration.

American industry has invested heavily in executive training programs for middle management. Some corporations have planned and set up their own training programs; others have utilized the services of graduate schools of business. So far, American higher education has made only a token effort to organize similar programs on campus or to pay for outside courses for promising college or university administrators. The presidents of our colleges and universities must now give attention to training programs for administrators, both those beginning careers and those in the junior and middle ranks of administration. It is no longer practical for presidents and other senior academic officers to pick up likely administrators on the basis of chance observation or occasional reference.[1]

Internships in various campus offices offer an opportunity to increase understanding of how the institution functions, office by office, and in the whole. Seminars are another avenue for interesting the new or not-so-new administrator in the potential of his job and of increasing his understanding of the institution. Internships and other educational programs can, of course, be combined in various ways. The aim of such programs should be to present a wide range of subjects in a way that will excite the interest of students to bring high intellectual qualities to bear on institutional problems. The curriculum must deal with the current problems affecting higher education noted earlier in this book, as well as consider how decisions are made and authority exercises within the college or university as an institution for the continuation and improvement of our society.

The faculty for a seminar or institute on the problems associated with administering a college or university under today's conditions could be drawn from the ranks of working administrators and from academic departments such as history, business, law, political science, and psychology. Responsibility for putting on the program might be assigned to a center for the study of higher education, if available on campus, to a professional school, or to the academic dean in a smaller institution. By broadening and quickening the interest and perception of the administrative staff and updating their competence in the discipline of higher education, there will be benefits for all concerned beyond the goal of personnel improvement.

Administrative officers with longer tenure could benefit from study leaves at other colleges and universities and from the opportunity for refreshment and self-study provided in an administrative sabbatical. There is the problem of sparing men who are important to on-going operations for the considerable periods of time which would be required, but such a program would pay dividends to the institution and could be worked out in such a way as to reduce the short-term manpower loss to a minimum. People get sick and temporarily worn out. It is then demonstrated that they are not indispensable, often to the dismay of the officer concerned. Time away from the job, in addition to vacations, is feasible if carefully arranged. Even if it is difficult to schedule time off for administrative training during the academic year, it should be possible in most institutions to sponsor summer institutes for administrators along the lines of executive training programs in business. A program of four to six weeks' duration would offer an opportunity for an in-depth study of business and financial theory as well as the subject matter of higher education. Programs of such duration and scope have not been considered feasible to date. However, academic corporations are growing even faster than industrial corporations, and the need for management training is at least as great. Executive training programs need not be a monopoly of the business schools. They could be put on with the assistance of the staffs of centers for the study of higher education, of junior college leadership centers, or by specially recruited faculty at off-campus conference centers.

One may ask whether the present trend toward proliferation of institutes, workshops, and training programs according to administrative specialty is the right way to improve leadership in the academic community. The Institute for College and University Administrators might consider programs which unite various administrative specialties in order to discuss their common problems. Presidents, deans, chairmen, business and financial officers, even trustees, can learn from their colleagues in other branches of administrative service, and their universities or colleges will be strengthened accordingly. The various associations of colleges and universities might usefully serve as conference centers. No formal association machinery is required: the Ivy League colleges and universities, for example, might create an *ad hoc* committee to administer such a program. The important ingredients are mutual need, mutual interest, and mutual financing from regular budgetary allocations. The expenses of programs to improve the quality of administration will have to be added to operating budgets. It is not realistic to expect outside financial help to continue to support programs in which the chief benefit accrues to the operations of the institution concerned. Regular budgetary allocations for these purposes are an indispensable investment in the sound growth of colleges and universities.

THE ROLE OF ADMINISTRATORS IN HIGHER EDUCATION

Arthur S. Adams has noted that the problems associated with administration in higher education are "deeply sensed but not completely identified."[2] The art or science of administration in higher education has apparently been considered to be a subjective mystery known only to its practitioners *in situ*. It has not been the subject of systematic study and observation.[3] A better understanding of the role of the administrator is important for the sound development of our colleges and universities as these institutions grow in size, complexity, expense, and in areas of service. Webster's *New Collegiate Dictionary* defines "administration" as "dispensing or tendering to another." This is the subsidiary or supporting role in which administration is often cast. A second definition by Webster is "the performance of the executive duties of an institution, business or the like." An administrator is both servant and executive.

A good administrator is a professional in his own right. Abraham Flexner's classic criteria of a profession[4] apply to the modern college and university administrator: (1) intellectual operations coupled with large individual responsibilities; (2) raw materials drawn from science and learning; (3) practical application; (4) an educationally communicable technique; (5) tendency toward self-organization; and (6) increasingly altruistic motivation.

The effective modern administrator in higher education is not a professor who is too tired to teach, an alumnus who has failed in some other occupation, or someone who has drifted into what he conceives to be a comfortable low-pressure job. He is a person with special training in the increasingly complicated task of directing and organizing the energies of an educational corporation, and he should be prepared to keep up with the latest thinking in the discipline of academic administration as it develops in higher education. The competent administrator must not only understand his "subject," but must know how to apply what he learns with practical effect and take responsibility for his decisions. He must be able to communicate to colleagues, faculty, students, alumni, and trustees the nature of the problems he faces and the rationale for the methods he employs to solve them. He will gain insights and experience from his professional association with colleagues who perform similar roles in other institutions.

When officers of instruction, administration, and research understand the importance and professional responsibility of their several roles in the conduct of an institution's affairs, all will serve the institution better. Too often today the different elements of the academic community appear to be in conflicting, rather than in complementary, roles. One way to restore a sense of unity in the search for truth, the meaning and purpose of a university, is to achieve a better understanding of the responsibility of students, teachers, trustees, and administrators for the direction and excellence of the college or university in which they "reside." The old French Estates-General may provide a useful analogy for a better understanding of this relationship. The students comprise one "estate"; the faculty, another; and the trustees and officers of administration, still another. It does no injustice to any one estate to recognize the distinctions among them.

A student has a personal objective in mind when he matriculates; he also assumes his share of responsibility for the intellectual program and the good name of his college or university. In this respect he represents his institution and has the right and duty to understand its policies and participate, where appropriate, in their formulation. A faculty member has individual goals and professional loyalties; he also assumes his share of responsibility for the reputation and intellectual tradition of the institution. As a member of the faculty body, he also participates, where appropriate, in the formulation and carrying out of academic policy.

If the trustees were to resign and the administration which acts in their name to wither away, a state often viewed as utopian by other members of the academic community, the educational enterprise would fly apart. Long-range planning and on-going continuity in the formulation and administration of academic policy must be the responsibility of the trustees and administrators. They have the opportunity to focus their thoughts and energies primarily, rather than secondarily, as in the case of the students and faculty, on the well-being and development of the institution they serve.

Each estate has rights and responsibilities within a university. Recognition of these rights and responsibilities is at the heart of an effective educational enterprise. The president and his administrative colleagues must initiate the process of clarifying student, faculty, and administrative roles *vis-a-vis* the institution. To do this, he must inform, trust, and make full use of his colleagues in the administration — not just at the senior level, but in the middle and lower ranks as well. They are constantly dealing with students, faculty, alumni and others; and they, too, can be teachers about the university. A university is not only a place where individuals teach and learn. It is in a larger sense the product of the *esprit* of an academic community, in which a vital ingredient is able, well-informed leadership in all ranks of administration.

Administration thus broadly conceived does not imply that Webster's first definition of administration as service is out of date. A portion of the president's time and that of his associates will be devoted to supporting the great roles of study, teaching, and research. But the additional transitive meaning of administration in the sense of running the institution, of seeing that its goals are clear, and that it makes progress toward these goals — this executive function — is the primary responsibility of the administrator in higher education.

Good communication within the administration is an important responsibility of the college or university president. At the top the means for good communication are at hand. The president and his deans are members and often chairmen of faculty groups. The departmental chairmen, who serve both as officers of administration and instruction, need only keep clear their respective roles in order to insure a free flow of information. The cabinet officers of the central administration, if we are considering a large university, have weekly meetings with the deans. There usually exist faculty councils or senates for the top echelon of the administrative and faculty estates, and the departmental faculty meeting is a universal source of information about the academic thrust of the institution. These normal lines of communication may be poor, but that is because of human failure, not faulty organization. However, the middle rank or junior administrator may be left out of the communication network. He may not be invited to departmental faculty meetings and does not attend the cabinet sessions or deans' meeting. He may have a seat on the university council by grace of a presidential appointment, but the really interesting problems of the institution are not debated but only ratified in such a forum. The result is that these officers may exist in limbo, or think they do. They cannot interpret and properly serve the goals and objectives of the university unless they have a part in the formulation of institutional policy.

SPECIALIZATION WITHIN ACADEMIC ADMINISTRATION

It is customary to speak of "areas of administration" in higher education. The new edition of the book on university business and accounting practices by the American Council on Education, lists four such areas: (1) Instruction and research; (2) Business and financial operations; (3) Student services; and (4) Alumni and public relations (including "development"). Such a listing suggests that the people who work in each of these areas are somehow engaged in separate and distinct careers. Although there are areas of special competence in administration requiring special training, the executive function in a university is indivisible. Academic administration describes the work of all offices of administration in a university. Each administrator is committed to the advancement of the university as a whole. His primary working concern, in contrast with teacher, researcher, student, trustee, alumnus, or interested member of the public, is the evolution of the enterprise.

With specialization there should be recognition of the importance of each specialty to the university as a whole. There is no hierarchy which separates officers of administration who work in academic departments or in areas that are closely associated with the provost and the central administration from those who work in the business area of the university. Specialization and special training, if required, are elements of the job, not something which sets one group of administrators apart from another. The university will have a number of officers of administration who are part-time administrators. For example, the assistant dean of a school may also be a part-time teacher, or the director of the office of research may himself be engaged in research projects for the university. It is important for these officers to recognize that their time in administration is as important as that in other aspects of university activity.

The departmental chairman is in an especially difficult position. He is primarily a teacher, but also an officer of administration. In this respect he is in exactly the same relationship to the president, trustees, and the university as a whole, as is the budget director, the business manager, or any other full-time officer of administration. It is difficult to wear two hats: to view the university as an individual teacher with a loyalty to subject matter, and as an administrator with a loyalty to the institution but this is what is required of the administrative officer no matter how specialized his background and training or how small a portion of his total working time may be devoted to administration in the university.

The work of a university requires a division of responsibility in service to a common goal. There should be no central administration separate and distinct from administrative service to teachers and students. The president and his principal aides in academic and business administration should regard their roles as in close support of school and departmental administration, while at the same time the departmental officers should understand the importance of the flow of sound and timely information to the central coordinating officers.

An example is the area of accounting. The department, no matter how small, will be spending money and will require accounts on which it can draw. The departmental chairman managing his accounts with the university is like an individual who has a credit account with a bank. He draws his checks, keeps his own records, and when the statement comes from the bank (in the case of the university, from the central accounting office), reconciles his statement with central accounting records. This is an example of team operation. Keeping central records depends on informed and prompt action at the departmental level while at the same time the departmental officers must have the sympathetic help and understanding of the experts in the central accounting office. The personnel office, to cite another example, is not a remote center where a departmental officer goes when he needs to hire personnel. The actual personnel function must be close to the job. The university personnel office is there to coordinate, to provide information, and generally to make the whole operation go smoothly.

The Significance of a New Order of Excellence in Academic Administration

The improvement of academic administration as a profession is sometimes interpreted as a call for the perpetuation of bureaucracy in higher education. Henry David Aiken writes of

. . . the appalling menace of full-time university executives and their appendages, who indeed make a mission of administration and whose relations to what goes on in the classroom or the laboratory, not to mention the dormitory or the common room, are not sufficiently developed to be called ceremonial.

He criticizes the president of a great university for

. . . his suave defense of the burgeoning, immensely costly administrative bureaucracy, with its lunatic hierarchy of trustees, presidents and vice presidents, chancellors and provosts and department 'heads,' its subtly influential administrative and secretarial assistants for whom frequently not only the students but the ordinary faculty members are figures in a committee report. . . .[5]

Professor Aiken's concern is understandable. This "view from the outside" is not unrealistic. The answer, however, is not to damn the president's efforts to run a modern college or university but to help him win the staff and administrative support which will enable him to lead his institution while maintaining personal contact with students and faculty.

The call for a new order of excellence at all levels of academic administration is better interpreted as a means of liberating college and university presidents from bureaucratic mediocrity. When such reform occurs presidents have time to consider the objectives their institutions *should* serve and the trends which are shaping this development. To lift an institution from a bureaucratic morass, an academic president and his senior associates need a staff capable of sharing an understanding of the institution's goals, resources, and operating methods. Higher education is moving to the center of American life. It now must attract not only the ablest teachers and researchers but young administrators of the first quality, who prefer service in higher education to employment in industry or labor organizations or government. The industrial analogy need not suggest a threat to academic excellence, but rather an opportunity for academic excellence to prosper despite the great pressures which society is placing upon our colleges and universities.

FINANCING AND FISCAL CONTROL

In its first 100 years the Office of Education (now in the Department of Health, Education and Welfare) expended $11.3 billions. In fiscal 1967 and 1968 appropriations to the Office of Education ran at the annual rate of $4 billion, and this rate of fiscal support may be expected to increase. A substantial portion of this flood of federal money will go to higher education. Does this signify an end to the problem of financing American higher education? Is it an opportunity for tired presidents, trustees, and their staffs to stop worrying about where the money is coming from to meet the tremendous needs of their institutions?

This new federal money, a high level of private support for higher education, and a gain in state appropriations are definitely encouraging to the academic community. Needed facilities are going up; deferred capital needs are being met; libraries are better supplied with materials and more modern in services; student aid, including loan and work programs, is benefiting greater numbers of students; colleges and universities are able to branch out into adult and continuing education and are able to assist in educational aspects of the economic opportunity programs; faculty and students are participating in academic research as never before. However, budgets are scarcely in balance. The search for new money continues unabated to meet the expense of new facilities, make up for insufficient overhead recovery on contracts, and cover fringe expenses on additions to the curriculum — to cite a few of the costs of educational progress.

It is possible to be overwhelmed by the pervasive fiscal plight of our affluent colleges and universities. The demands of society on these institutions today are greater than the willingness of society to render the necessary financial support. These pressures are likely to continue until the economy recedes, and then our colleges and universities will have other, perhaps more difficult, financial problems.

Each educational administration must set its house in order from a business and financial point of view. Able officers who know and understand the educational opportunities of their college or university can play a leading role in trimming sails without loss of headway. They can be most effective when the chief academic officers are interested in and reasonably knowledgeable about the business and financial operation of the institution. Proper information on budgets and expenses communicated to teachers, students, trustees, alumni, and the public will help all parties hold down expenses and will encourage them to take into account the financial dimensions of new projects.

Recently, there has been considerable interest in comparing financial accounting practices in the United States with those in the foreign countries in which our business corporations are now heavily investing. In one such study, a spokesman for the Lockheed Aircraft Corporation cited the U. S. emphasis on management planning, based upon budgets and forecasting techniques, as the most significant difference in financal accounting practices in the United States and Europe.[6] Lockheed, for example, prepares a ten-year master plan, a combination market survey and financial forecast, with contributions from university consultants and other outside experts, as well as from internal sources. The corporation then prepares a series of five-year forecasts by operating divisions. The first year of the five-year forecast becomes the management budget for the coming year. When a budget or longer forecast indicates a declining volume of sales, an undesirable profit rate, a shortage of cash, or an unwarranted build-up of inventories, management can act to prevent the trouble. Historical financial data from the balance sheet and income statements are then compared with the forecast and budget as a measure of reliability and performance.

U. S. business managers demand a year-end performance report without waiting for the books to be closed and the later audited financial report. In contrast, European managers often wait until 17 months after the close of the fiscal year for such data. This emphasis on planning, forecasting, and availability of the very latest economic and financial data is an American phenomenon. Why? Dudley Brown of Lockheed suggests that the U. S. emphasis reflects our national impatience with the past and our eagerness for the future. As a people we prefer to ask "How well are we going to do?" rather than "How well have we done?". We are a pragmatic people. We are interested in having good historical data but more as a basis for planning and possibly changing things in the future than as a record of performance.

In many ways U. S. academic managements have operated in the "European" tradition with respect to data about their institutions. Budgets and forecasts have been crude or unavailable and not comparable with actual results. And actual financial results are often available too late to help in budget preparation, let alone longer financial forecasting as suggested in the "academic program budget" described in Chapter I. In the area of business planning, academic leaders must become as astute as their colleagues in business. Otherwise, our great educational corporations will continue to drift into financial difficulty and plans to improve academic performance will be jeopardized. Here is the opportunity for an academic "managerial revolution."[7] The object of this revolution is to free the academic community so that it can attain optimum productivity, not to convert it into a business house and thus put a premium on mediocrity as

Veblen feared.[8] Uncertainty or fear about the financial future of an institution poisons the atmosphere and affects teaching and research. Long-range planning based on sound data permits optimum allocation of money and an atmosphere of confidence in the future of the institution.

To date, our colleges and universities have tended to look inward at their own needs rather than outward at the general needs of higher education. Now academic presidents are beginning to study the educational needs of states and regions and how the goals of their colleges and universities fit into these broader educational objectives. There are now fifty state councils for allocating federal grants; associations of colleges, particularly in the private sector, are increasing in number; and the regional interstate compacts have now been supplemented by the Compact for Education which in July, 1966 formed the Educational Commission of the States. We are developing a system of higher education through councils, compacts, and associations without subjecting individual colleges and universities to state or national control. We are working toward a national goal in higher education without imposing a ministry of education on our academic leaders. This delicate and difficult task of coordination without control is a proper subject for study and research. Our colleges and universities, which are doing so much to study "extracurricular" problems of the world, should consider the opportunity for self-study as they plan individually and in council for the future.

THE ROLE OF THE COLLEGE AND UNIVERSITY IN AMERICAN LIFE

Higher education is seen by its many "users" in different roles. Student, teacher, researcher or research customer, parent, alumnus, business or government hiring officer—each focuses on a particular aspect of higher education in America. There is a broader cast to the "Why?" of American higher education. Our colleges and universities are more than giant service corporations honing the intellect of the young and not so young, codifying what we choose to classify as "knowledge" and adding, often in painfully small drops, to the deposit of what man has found out about himself and the world about him. These institutions, as well or better than any other element of society, can influence the quality of the end product—twentieth century man himself.

Two social scientists, Bernard Berelson and Gary A. Steiner, have asked how we might characterize this mid-twentieth century "man of the behavioral sciences".[9] They note that:

> In his quest for satisfaction, this man is not just a seeker of truth, but of deceptions, of himself as well as others. . . . Thus, he adjusts his social perception to fit not only the objective reality but also what suits his wishes and his needs . . . ; he tends to remember what fits his needs and expectations . . . or what he thinks others will want to hear . . . ; he not only works for what he wants, but *wants what he has to work for.* (emphasis supplied).

Berelson and Steiner are not seeking to grade modern man in relation to medieval man or ancient man. They classify their book as "an inventory of . . . the present state of scientific knowledge about human behavior."[10] However, their findings amount to an indictment of the material man of the mid-twentieth century.

Our colleges and universities have a reponsibility not only to cater to the needs of twentieth-century man but to help him recast his needs in terms of his heritage, responsibility, and opportunity. The greatest challenge to our academic leaders is not to make their institutions more efficient in serving the apparent goals of society, but to make these institutions strong enough to stand for the truth, regardless of popularity or utility, and through them to offer a new dimension to the dreams and aspirations of individual Americans.

People who "want what they work for" are doomed to a closed life no matter how facile, efficient, and knowledgeable they may become. Education can liberate them *to work for what they want.* The goal of higher education is to define the potential of life so that individuals may aspire to live abundantly and responsibly. Achievement of this goal requires inspired and competent academic leadership on the campuses of America.

1. A 1965 research study by the U.S. Office of Education of business management of U.S. colleges and universities notes that most of the chief business officers of the nation's colleges and universities gained their experience outside the academic world. Reported in "Higher Education in National Affairs," November 25, 1966.

2. Raymond F. Howes (Ed.), *Toward Better Preparation of College and University Administrators, op. cit.,* p. 33.

3. "The basic problems of academic administration have been so infrequently assayed, that the lack of knowledge constitutes a major deficiency in their functioning." Neil Gross, "Organizational Lag in American Universities," *Harvard Educational Review,* 33 (1963), pp. 69-70. Quoted in Betsy Ann Olive, "The Administration of Higher Education: A Bibliographical Survey," *Administrative Science Quarterly* (March 1967), p. 675.

4. Abraham Flexner, Is Social Work a Profession? (New York, N.Y.: N.Y. School of Philanthropy, 1915). (An address before the National Conference of Charities and Correction, Baltimore, Maryland, May 17, 1915).

5. Henry David Aiken, "The American University: Part 1," *The New York Review of Books,* October 20, 1966.

6. Dudley E. Browne, "Differences Between U.S. and Foreign Reporting," *Financial Executive* (January 1963), pp. 20-23, 43.

7. Glen E. Brooks and Francis E. Rourke, *The Managerial Revolution in Higher Education, op. cit.*

8. Thorsten Veblen, *The Higher Learning in America* (New York, N.Y.: Hill & Wang, 1954, copyright 1918).

9. Bernard Berelson and Gary A. Steiner, *Human Behavior. An Inventory of Scientific Findings* (New York, N.Y.: Harcourt Brace & World, Inc., 1964), conclusion.

10. *Ibid.,* Introduction.

Appendix

The Phillips Interns in Academic Administration were employees at the "home" institutions listed below when they were accepted to spend up to one full academic year at one or more of the "host" institutions. In addition, interns were accepted from government service and private employment.

List of home institutions

Agricultural & Technical College of North Carolina
Alabama State College
Colby College
Danbury State College
Davidson College
Dickinson College
Duke University
Emory University
Florida State University
Foothill College (Los Altos, California)
Fresno State College
Georgetown University
Harvard Business School
Hofstra University
Idaho State University
Kent State University
Michigan State University
Montana State University
North Carolina State University, Raleigh
Northern Illinois University
Ohio Wesleyan University
Orange County Community College
San Francisco State College
Southern Illinois University
Texas Southern University
Tulane University
University of California, Berkeley
University of Denver
University of Idaho
University of Illinois
University of Michigan
University of New Hampshire
University of South Florida
University of Virginia
University of Washington
University of Wisconsin
Western Reserve University

List of host institutions

American University
Barnard College
Boston University
Brooklyn College
Brown University
Chatham College
City College of New York
Claremont Graduate School and University Center
Columbia University
Cornell University
Dartmouth College
DePauw University
Duke University
Hamilton College
Harvard University
Howard University
Indiana State College
Indiana University
Michigan State University
Ohio State University
Oregon State University
Pennsylvania State University
Princeton University
Rutgers University
San Francisco State College
Sarah Lawrence College
Smith College
Stanford University
University of California, Berkeley
University of California, Los Angeles
University of California, Riverside
University of Chicago
University of Houston
University of Illinois
University of Iowa
University of Michigan
University of Minnesota
University of New Hampshire
University of North Carolina
University of North Carolina, Greensboro
University of Pennsylvania
University of Rhode Island
University of Rochester
University of Texas
University of Washington
University of Wisconsin